HOUGHTON MIFFLIN HARCOURT

JOURNEYS

Road Map to Success

Write-In Reader
Grade 1 Vol. 1

Printed in the U.S.A.

ISBN: 978-0-547-25403-6

123456789 - 0877 - 17 16 15 14 13 12 11 10 09

HOUGHTON MIFFLIN HARCOURT
School Publishers

Contents

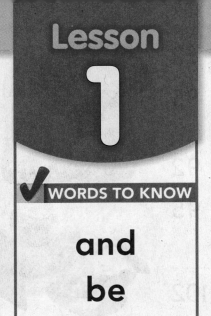

✓ WORDS TO KNOW

and

be

help

play

My Pals

Read the sentence.

Write the new word.

1 Cat-cat can **play**.

play

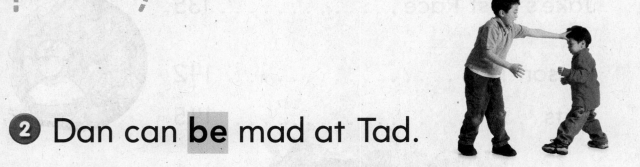

2 Dan can **be** mad at Tad.

be

3 Nan can **help** Dad.

help

4 Sam, Cam, **and** Tam sat.

and

Read the words in the word box.
Write the word under the picture.

mad	cat
mat	dad

1

_____

- - - - - - - - - - -

_____

2

WELCOME

_____

- - - - - - - - - - -

_____

3

_____

- - - - - - - - - - -

_____

4

_____

- - - - - - - - - - -

_____

4

Pam and Fan

by Emma Riba

Mad, mad, mad!

Mad, mad, mad, mad!

Pam can **be** mad, mad, mad.

Fan is sad.
Sad, sad, sad!

Can Pam help Fan?
Can Fan help Pam?

Pam and Fan can!
Pam and Fan can play.

Check the answer.

1 **Who is Pam?**

☐ a girl   ☐ a dog

2 **How is Pam feeling at first?**

☐ sad   ☐ mad

3 **What do Pam and Fan do?**

☐ play   ☐ nap

Write about Pam.

_____

- -

4 **Pam is** _____ .

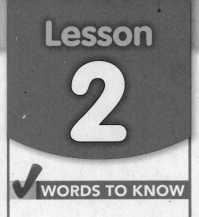

✓ WORDS TO KNOW

he

for

look

what

Read the sentence.
Write the new word.

① Is **he** mad?

he

② Did Pam **look** at it?

look

12

3 It is sad **for** Mip.

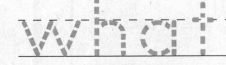

4 Tap, tap, tap! See **what** it is.

Read the words in the word box.
Write the word under the picture.

pin	pit
tip	fin

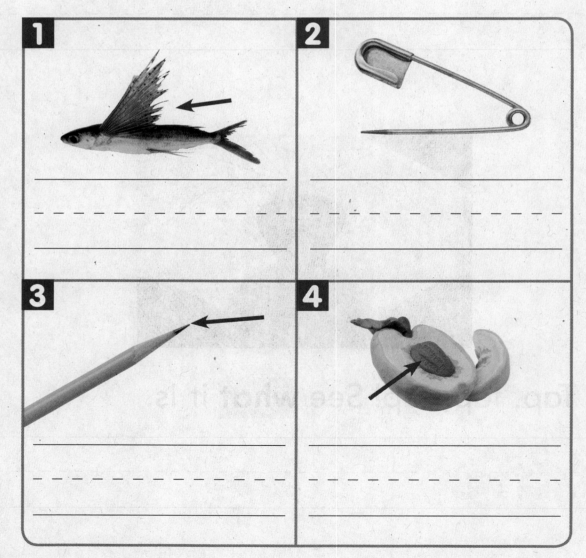

1

——————————

- - - - - - - - - -

——————————

2

——————————

- - - - - - - - - -

——————————

3

——————————

- - - - - - - - - -

——————————

4

——————————

- - - - - - - - - -

——————————

Mag Big Sis Dad Tim Pip

Pip Can Help

by Janice Winfield

RIP, RAP, BAM!

Mag hid.

Big Sis ran in.

Bam, bam, bam!
Dad ran in.

Dad sat with Mag.

Mag had a sip.

Bam! Bam!

Tim ran in.

Look **what** Tim had **for** Mag.

He had Pip for Mag!

Pip can help Mag.

Zzzzzz.

Check the answer.

1 Who hid?

☐ Big Sis ☐ Mag

2 What did Dad give Mag?

☐ a sip ☐ a nap

3 What did Tim have?

☐ a nap ☐ Pip

Write about a storm.

_____

4 A storm is _____.

Lesson

3

✓ WORDS TO KNOW

do

funny

no

they

At School

Read the sentence.

Write the new word.

1 Sal had **no** bag.

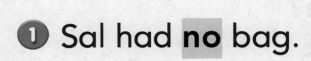

no

2 Lib can **do** it!

do

3 It is not bad.

Can **they** can fix it?

they

4 His pal Rob is **funny**.

funny

Read the words in the word box.

Write the words under the picture.

dot	log
mop	top

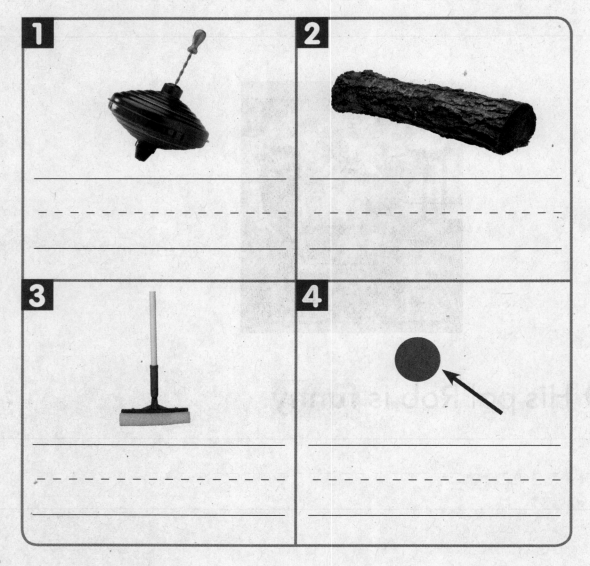

1

_____

- - - - - - - - - - -

_____

2

_____

- - - - - - - - - - -

_____

3

_____

- - - - - - - - - - -

_____

4

_____

- - - - - - - - - - -

_____

Bad Cat

by Marvin Hampton

HERBERT HOOVER ELEMENTARY

NO PETS AT SCHOOL

Dot is a **funny** cat.

What if Dot got in?
Can Dot **do** it?

Dot did it!

Dot got in.

Dot ran.

Dot ran on.

Got him!

Can cats go in?

No, they can not!

 **Look Back and Respond**  Read Together

Check the answer.

1 **Where is Dot?**

☐ at school

☐ at home

2 **What happened first?**

☐ Dot got in.

☐ Dot ran on a hot pot.

3 **What happened last?**

☐ A lady said, "Cat!"

☐ A teacher got Dot.

Write about Dot.

_____

4 **Dot is** _____.

all
does
here
who

My Neighbors

Read the sentence.
Write the new word.

1 Pals can **all** fit on top.

_a̶l̶l̶_

2 Meg met Lin **here**.

_h̶e̶r̶e̶_

③ Big Ben **does** not let Ted win.

does

④ I see **who** it is!

who

Read the words in the word box.
Write the word under the picture.

hen	red
ten	bed

1

2

3

4

Dex

by Roberto Gómez

It is big **here**.
Dex **does** not fit in.

Who can help Dex?

Hens can not.

Pigs can not.

Dex is not a pig.

Dogs can not.
All the dogs yap at him.

Dex met Len.

Len led him here.

 It is not bad here.
It is not bad at all!

Look Back and Respond

Check the answer.

1 How do you know Dex is a duck?

☐ from the words

☐ from the picture

2 Where is the title?

☐ on the first page

☐ on the last page

3 On page 38, which dog is yapping?

☐ the brown dog

☐ the gray dog

Write about Dex's home.

4 His home is _____ .

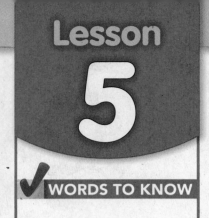

✓ **WORDS TO KNOW**

friend

good

hold

many

At the Zoo

Read the sentence.
Write the new word.

1 The big cat runs with **many** cubs.

2 Yum, yum, yum! It is **good**!

good

3 His **friend** has bugs on him.

friend

4 The pen can **hold** a big pig.

hold

Read the words in the word box.
Write the word under the picture.

cut	bud
mug	sun

1

2

3

4

Sal

by Paola Rizzi

Sal begs for a pet.

His mom had **many** pets.

His mom is not a fan.

Sal runs in.
Fun, fun, fun!

Is it a pet?
It is big. It is fun.
But it is not a pet.

It is a big cat!
Sal can not sit on it.
It is not a pet.

It is a big cub!
It can hug Sal.
No cub hugs for Sal!

Dad has a box.
What did it **hold**?
It is not a big cub.
But it is a **good friend**!

 **Look Back and Respond**  Read Together

Check the answer.

1 **What does Sal want?**

☐ a pet

☐ a sister

2 **Where did Sal go?**

☐ to the vet

☐ to the zoo

3 **Who went with Sal?**

☐ his mom

☐ his dad

Write about an animal Sal saw.

4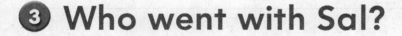

_____

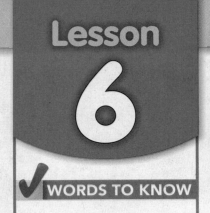
✓ **WORDS TO KNOW**

away

come

every

said

Read the sentence.

Write the new word.

1 Run, Miss!

Run **away**!

2 Who will **come** to fix him?

3 "It is big!" **said** Pig.

"It is bad!"

said

4 Jack and Jill go up **every** hill.

every

Read the words in the word box.
Write the word under the picture.

sock	kiss
bell	egg

1

_____

- - - - - - - - - - - -

_____

2

_____

- - - - - - - - - - - -

_____

3

_____

- - - - - - - - - - - -

_____

4

_____

- - - - - - - - - - - -

_____

Tom

Run, Run, Run!

Jack

by Edith Rivera

Tom got set.

Jack got set.

Run, Tom! Run, Jack!

Run, run, run!

Away Jack ran.

"I am quick," **said** Jack.

"I will win!"

"**Come** on!" said Tom.

"Huff, huff, puff.

I will jog up **every** hill.

I will pass him yet!"

"Tom is not quick," said Jack.

"I can win in a jiff."

Jack sat. Jack had a nap.

As Jack sat, Tom ran up.

"Rats!" said Jack. "Bad luck!"

"It is not luck," said Tom.

"I am not quick, but I did not quit!"

Check the answer.

1 **Who is Jack?**

☐ a bunny   ☐ a turtle

2 **Is Jack quick?**

☐ yes   ☐ no

3 **Why did Tom win?**

☐ Tom is quick.

☐ Tom did not quit.

Do you like Jack? Tell why.

4 _____

How Do Animals Talk?

**Read the sentence.
Write the new word.**

① An **animal** can tell us if it is mad.

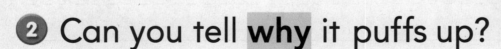

animal

② Can you tell **why** it puffs up?

why

3 Lots **of** ducks quack.

of

4 Hiss! It can **make** us run.

make

Read the words in the word box.
Write the word under the picture.

crab	brick
truck	drum

1

_____

- - - - - - - - - - - -

_____

2

_____

- - - - - - - - - - - -

_____

3

_____

- - - - - - - - - - - -

_____

4

_____

- - - - - - - - - - - -

_____

Tell Cat!

by Megan Linke

"Quack, quack, quack," said Duck.
"Quack, quack! Quack, quack!"
But Cat did not see **why**.

"Crick, crick, crick," said Bug.

"Crick, crick! Crick, crick!"

"Hum?" said Cat.

"Bick, bick, bick," said Pig.

"Bick, bick! Bick, bick!"

"Lots **of** mud!" said Cat.

"Pigs can **make** a mess."

"Grup, grup, grup," said Frog.

"Grup, grup! Grup, grup!"

"Frog is an odd **animal**," said Cat.

"Buzz, buzz, buzz," I said.
"Buzz, buzz! Buzz, buzz!"

"Ack!" huffed Cat. "It is wet, wet, wet!"

Well, we did tell him!

But he did not get it.

Check the answer.

1 What were the animals saying?

☐ where to get food

☐ that it may rain

2 Who said "Buzz, buzz"?

☐ Bird   ☐ Bee

3 Look at page 69.

What detail tells you it will rain?

☐ Cat   ☐ the clouds

Write about animal sounds.

4 What sound does a cat make?

_____

- - - - - - - - - - - - - - - - - - -

_____

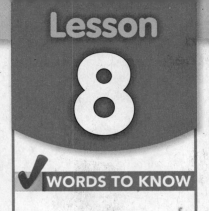

Lesson 8

✓ **WORDS TO KNOW**

her

now

our

she

Music Time!

Read the sentence.

Write the new word.

1 Can you clap like **she** can?

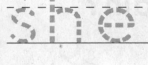

she

2 Glenn will pick up his bell **now**.

now

3 Rat-tat-tat!
Jan slaps **her** drum.

4 Miss Glass tells **our** class to "hit it"!

Read the words in the word box.
Write the word under the picture.

glass	plum
flag	black

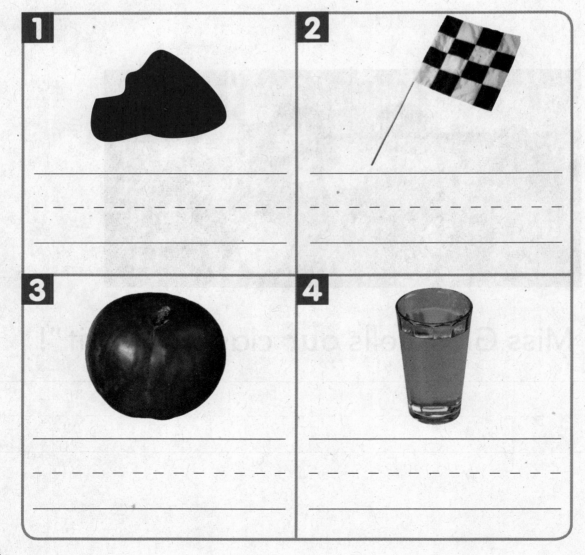

1

_____

- - - - - - - - - - - -

_____

2

_____

- - - - - - - - - - - -

_____

3

_____

- - - - - - - - - - - -

_____

4

_____

- - - - - - - - - - - -

_____

Pig   **Duck**   **Hess**   **Frog**   **El**

Hit It!

by Megan Linke

Pig trots up.

Clip, clop, clip!

Now Duck hops in.

Duck puffs. **She** trills.

Hess trots in back.

Clap, click! Click, clap!

Hess taps **her** drum.

Tat-tat! Pum-pum!

Our club is fun!

Plod! Clod! Crack!
Here is El. Ack!

Not fun! Not fun!

Run, run, run!

Look Back and Respond

Read Together

Check the answer.

1 Who starts the parade?

☐ Pig   ☐ Hess

2 Who ends the parade?

☐ Hess   ☐ El

3 When does Duck join in?

☐ after Hess   ☐ after Pig

Write about a parade you watched.

4 What did you see?

_____

- - - - - - - - - - - - - - - - - - -

_____

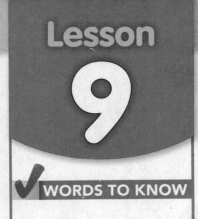

Lesson 9

✓ **WORDS TO KNOW**

after

read

was

write

Books and Writers

Read the sentence.
Write the new word.

1 Lib **was** in class.

was

2 Meg set it back **after** class.

after

3 Skip can **read** to his sis.

read

4 Stan will **write** on his pad.

Read the words in the word box.
Write the word under the picture.

skull	step
stem	snack

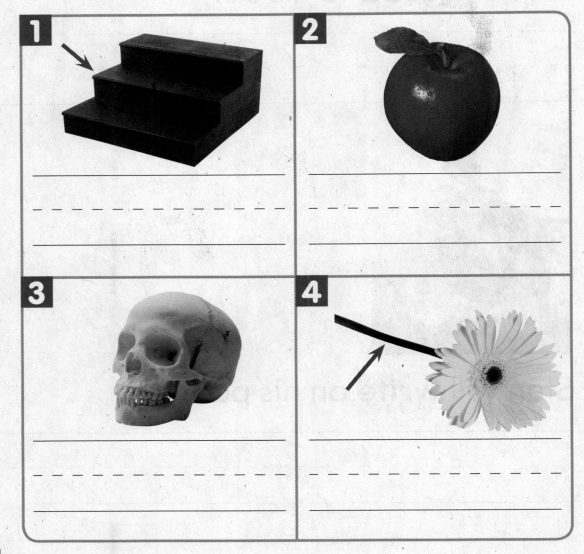

1.

2.

3.

4.

Scott and His Red Pen

by Paolo Rizzi

Scott sat in class.

Scott and his pals did the ABCs.

"It is fun, Miss Smitt," said Scott.

"But can I **read** yet?"

"Not yet, Scott," said Miss Smitt.

"But you will!"

It **was** not a snap.

But **after** a bit, Scott did it!

"It is fun, Dad," said Scott.

"But can I **write** yet?"

"Not yet, Scott," said his dad.

"But you will!"

Scott had his pad.

Scott had his red pen.

Scott had big plans, as well.

Today, Scott is a man.
Scott still has his red pen.
Scott is a big hit!

Read Together

Check the answer.

1 Why is "ABC" on page 85?

☐ to teach us our ABCs

☐ to show what Scott is learning

2 What is this story called?

☐ Scott and His Red Pen

☐ Scott

3 Look at page 88. Where is Scott?

☐ at the library

☐ at home

Write about a book you like.

4 _____

_____

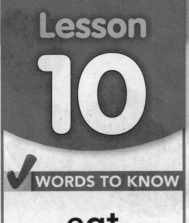

10

eat

give

put

take

Make It, Bake It!

Read the sentence.
Write the new word.

① Ben will **put** milk in it.

② Liz can **give** Grant a hand.

3 Dad will **take** it if it is not too hot.

4 If Mom cuts it, Jan can help **eat** it!

eat

Read the word in the word box.
Write the word under the picture.

hand	plant
lamp	milk

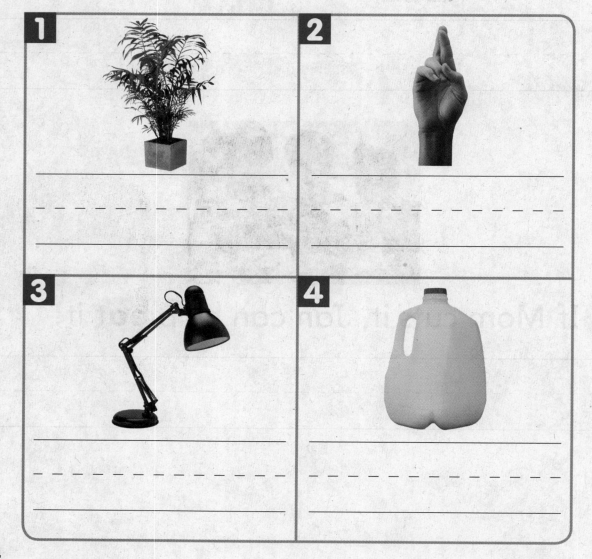

1.

2.

3.

4.

Cat   **Kid**   **Hen**   **Don**   **Ness**   **Pig**

Who Can Help Cat?

by Marc Vargas

Cat has a plan.

Who can help?

Kid can help Cat!
Kid will mix it up.

Don will fix the crust.

Don will **take** it and press it flat.

Ness can help, too.
Ness will **put** it in a pan.

Now Pig will help.
Pig will pick it up and **eat** it!

No, Pig!

Cat will cut it up.

And Cat will **give** a bit to all of us!

 **Look Back and Respond**  Read Together

Check the answer.

1 Where does the story take place?

☐ a kitchen ☐ a bedroom

2 Who wants help?

☐ Hen ☐ Cat

3 What does Pig try to do?

☐ eat the pie ☐ help Cat

Write about the story.

_____

- - - - - - - - - - - - - - - - - -

4 Who helps Cat? _____

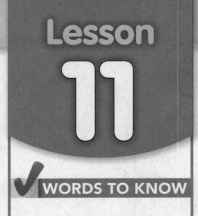

✓ **WORDS TO KNOW**

far
little
water
where

Sea Animals

Read the sentence.
Write the new word.

① This **little** crab sits on its rock.

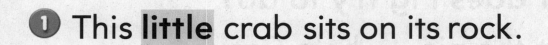

little

② Gulls can nest **far** up on cliffs.

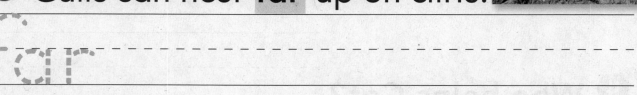

far

3 Can you tell **where** it is?

where

4 This **water** has lots in it!

water

Read the words in the word box.
Write the word under the picture.

bath	math
moth	path

1

_____

- - - - - - - - - - -

_____

2

_____

- - - - - - - - - - -

_____

3

_____

- - - - - - - - - - -

_____

4

$$\begin{array}{r} 3 \\ -\ 2 \\ \hline 1 \end{array}$$

_____

- - - - - - - - - - -

_____

Pup's Bath

by Diane Bird

Pup sat in his bath.

Mom sat with him.

"What is in this **water**?" asked Pup.

"Can you swim?" asked Mom.

Pup ducked.

Pup swam and swam.

Pup met lots of **little** pals.

Then Pup swam up to a big grin!

"Ack!" yelped Pup.

"Mom! **Where** is my mom?"

But Mom was **far** away.
Pup swam up, up, up.

Then Pup sat up.

"Mom!" yelled Pup.

"What a trip!"

Then his mom just picked him up.
"Off to bed," Mom said.

Look Back and Respond

Read Together

Check the answer.

1 **What is this text for?**

☐ to teach you

☐ to tell a story

2 **What is the story about?**

☐ Pup's bath time

☐ how to keep clean

3 **What scares Pup?**

☐ a bar of soap   ☐ a big turtle

Write about Pup's trip.

4 **What did he see?**

_____

- -

_____

Lesson 12

WORDS TO KNOW

✔

never

off

own

very

Animal Stories

Read the sentence.

Write the new word.

1 This fox will **never** catch a chill.

never

2 Hess has spots that will not rub **off**.

3 A chick will stick with its **own** mom.

own

4 This animal can chop logs **very** well.

very

Read the words in the word box.
Write the word under the picture.

chin	patch
check	chess

1. _____

2. _____

3. _____

4. _____

114

Al and Lop

by Megan Linke

This is Lop.

Lop did not like water **very** much.

But Lop had his tricks.

"Al!" yelled Lop.

"I have lots of pals!"

"Not as many as me!" yelled Al.

"Run and fetch them," yelled Lop.

"And we will see!"

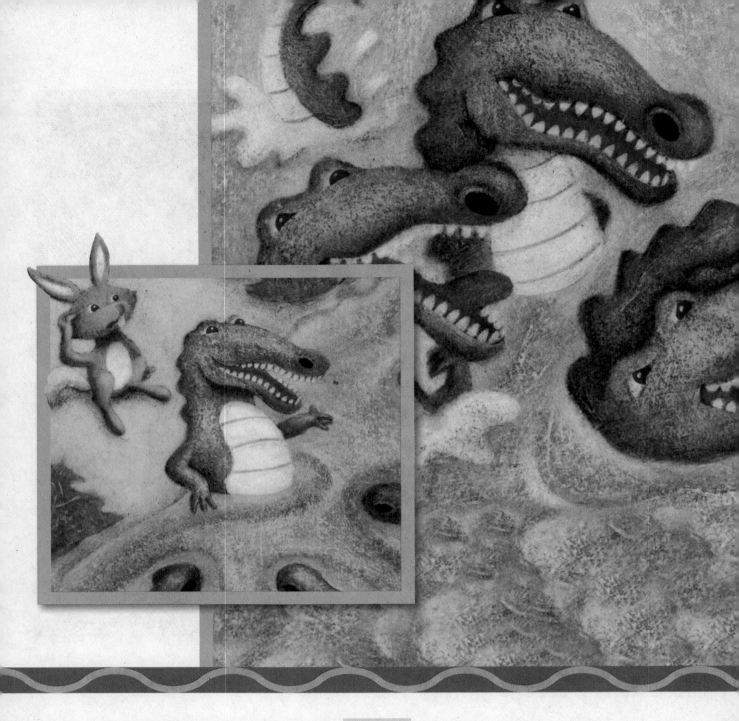

Al fetched his **own** pals.

But Lop just scratched his chin.

"This will **never** do!" clucked Lop.

"Set them up in a path."

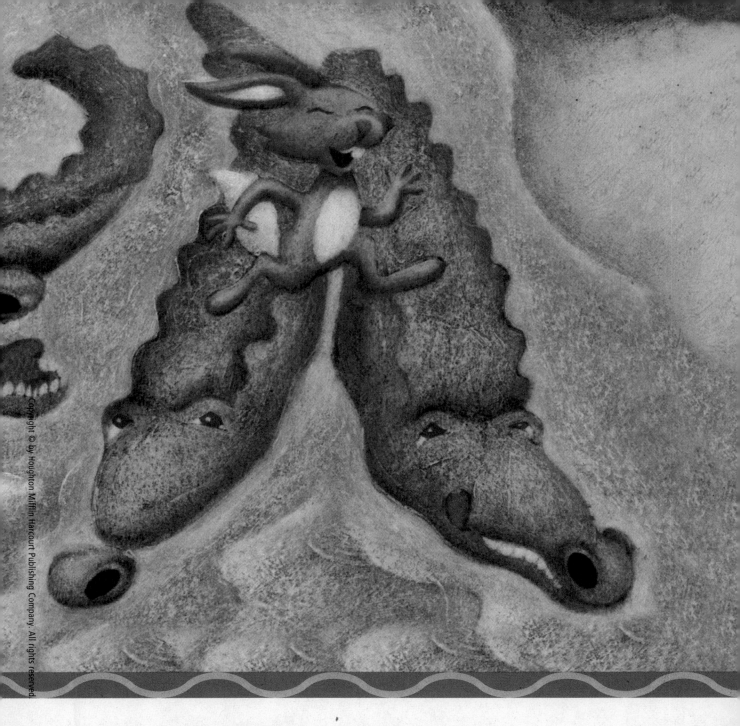

Al did.

Hop, hop, hop!

Lop ran on top of them.

Al's pals got mad, mad, mad!

Chomp! Al bit Lop as he got **off**.

Now all Lop has left is a puff of fluff!

Check the answer.

1 **Who do we see first?**

☐ Al   ☐ Lop

2 **What happened last?**

☐ Lop had to cross a river.

☐ Lop ran away.

3 **What happened after Al's pals got mad?**

☐ Al bit Lop.   ☐ Lop swam.

Write about the story.

4 **Do you think Lop's trick was smart?**

_____

- -

_____

✓ **WORDS TO KNOW**

down
goes
open
yellow

Seasons Changing

Read the sentence.
Write the new word.

① Red mixes in with **yellow**.

yellow

② Josh rushes **down** on his sled.

down

3 Buds **open** up.

open

4 Ash **goes** shell hunting with Jen.

goes

Read the words in the word box.
Write the word under the picture.

dish	ship
shell	cash

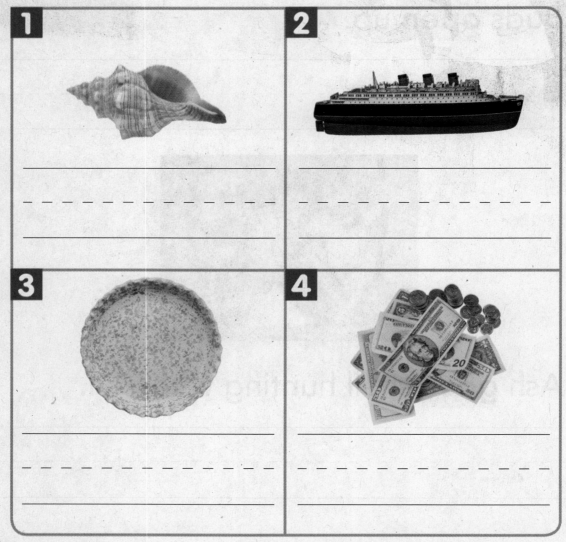

1

2

3

4

Max Has His Bath

by Emma Riba

Water gushes **down**.

It fills our path with mud.

Max has such fun splashing in that mess!

Then Max has to get his bath.

Max does not wish to have his bath.

But he must.

Now it is hot.

Max has **yellow** dust on him.

Phil pats his back.

Then Max **goes** in the tub!

In fall, twigs stick on Max.

I tell him, "Hop in, Max!"

But Max will not hop in.

I will pick him up and plop him in!

Now it is cold.

Max stands out in the **open**.

Slush melts on his back.

Now I will not ask Max.

Phil will not ask him.

But in a flash, Max will rush in.

Max is all set for his hot bath!

Look Back and Respond

Read Together

Check the answer.

1 **Why does Max have so many baths?**

☐ He is always hot.

☐ He is always a mess.

2 **Why does the girl pick Max up?**

☐ He will not hop into the tub.

☐ He is cold.

3 **What happens when Max is cold?**

☐ He does not need a bath.

☐ He wants a bath.

Write about Max in winter.

_____

- -

4 **Max likes his** _____ .

✓ WORDS TO KNOW

over

three

two

watch

Races

Read the sentence.
Write the new word.

1 Do not step **over** that tape yet!

2 Fans **watch** and clap.

3 The **three** kids hold eggs.

three

4 Ron held up his **two** hands.

two

133

Write a Word

Read the words in the word box.
Write the word under the picture.

snake	plane
tape	game

1 _____

2 _____

3 _____

4 _____

Jake's Best Race

Jake   Kim   Jane   **by Marc Vargas**

Three, **two**, one!

Jake shot off.

"I must win this race," hissed Jake.

"If not, it will not be fun."

Jake led at a quick pace.

But he did not **watch** the path.

Thump! Jake ran **over** a big rock.

Bam! Jake fell.

As Jake sat, Kim ran up.

"Face it, Jake," said Kim.
"You will not race."
Then Kate ran off.

As Kim left, Jane came up.

"My name is Jane," she said.

And she gave Jake a hand.

In the end, Jake did not win.
But he still had fun.
He had fun with his new pal, Jane.

Check the answer.

1 **Why can't Jake race?**

☐ because he fell

☐ because he had to go home

2 **Why was this Jake's "best" race?**

☐ because he won

☐ because he met Jane

3 **What will happen next?**

☐ Jake and Jane will be pals.

☐ Jake will finish the race.

Write about a race you were in.

4 _____

_____

✓ **WORDS TO KNOW**

eyes

long

or

walk

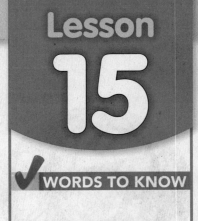

Animal Groups

Read the sentence.

Write the new word.

1 Fish can swim, but they can not **walk**.

walk

2 Snakes can eat mice **or** frogs.

or

3 Bugs can have **long** legs.

4 A cat's quick **eyes** help it hunt.

eyes

Write a Word

Read the words in the word box.

Write the word under the picture.

dime	kite
ice	mice

1
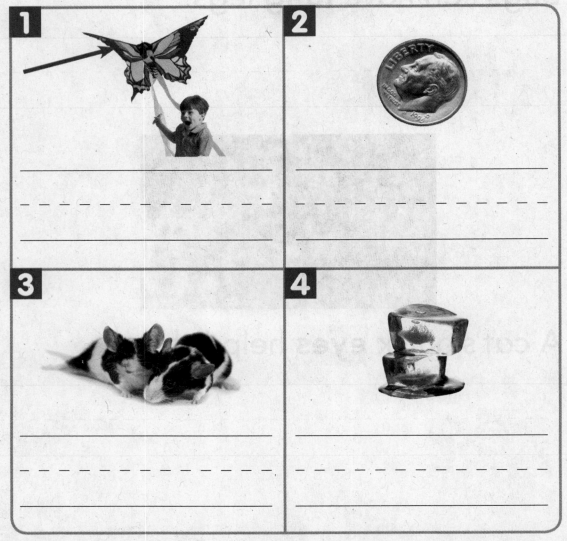

_____

- - - - - - - - - - -

_____

2

_____

- - - - - - - - - - -

_____

3

_____

- - - - - - - - - - -

_____

4

_____

- - - - - - - - - - -

_____

Cats

by Edith Rivera

Some say that cats have nine lives.

Cats do not have nine lives.

But cats can still do a lot!

Cats can be big **or** small.
But all cats can bite. Yikes!

This big cat is black with spots.
Its spots help it hide.

This cat sits on a **long** branch.

It has its **eyes** wide open.

If it spots an animal, it strikes!

This big cat hunts as well.
It can hunt mice, fish, and frogs.

Big cats can look like pets.
But it is not wise to pet them!
Never **walk** up to big cats.
It is best just to let them be.

Look Back and Respond

Check the answer.

1 **How are all cats the same?**

☐ They are the same size.

☐ They can all bite.

2 **How can big cats differ?**

☐ in color

☐ some have teeth, some don't

3 **If you see a big cat...**

☐ walk up to it.

☐ let it be.

Write about cats.

_____

4 **Cats are** _____.

Shutterstock. 2 (tr) © Shutterstock. 2 (b) © Rubberball Productions. 4 (tr) © PhotoDisc, Inc. 4 (bl) © Artville. 4 (tl) © PhotoDisc, Inc. 4 (br) © Rubberball Productions. 12 (t) © Getty Images/PhotoDisc. 12 (b) © Getty Images/PhotoDisc. 13 (t) © Corel Stock Photo Library. 13 (b) © Getty Images/PhotoDisc. 14 (tr) © PhotoDisc, Inc. 14 (tl) © Stockbyte. 14 (bl) © Photolink/PhotoDisc. 14 (br) © Image Club. 15 © Comstock. 17 © Classic PIO Images. 18 © PhotoDisc, Inc. 19 © Shutterstock. 24 (tl) © PhotoDisc, Inc. 24 (tr) © PhotoDisc, Inc. 24 (bl) © Stockbyte. 32 (t) © Getty Images/PhotoDisc. 33 (t) © Superstock. 33 (b) © Getty Images/PhotoDisc. 34 (tl) © Getty Images/PhotoDisc. 34 (tr) © Shutterstock. 42 (t) © Brand X Pictures. 42 (b) © Alamy. 43 (t) © Corel Stock Photo Library. 43 (b) © Digital Vision/Getty Images. 44 (tl) © PhotoDisc, Inc. 44 (tr) © PhotoDisc/Getty Images. 44 (br) © Eyewire/Getty Images. 54 (tl) © Artville. 54 (tr) © Getty Images/PhotoDisc. 54 (bl) © Brand X Pictures. 54 (br) © Digital Vision. 62 (t) © Corel Stock Photo Library. 62 (b) © PhotoDisc, Inc. 63 (t) © Corel Stock Photo Library. 63 (b) © Corel Stock Photo Library. 64 (tl) © Getty Images/PhotoDisc. 64 (tr) © PhotoDisc, Inc. 64 (br) © Getty Images/PhotoDisc. 64 (bl) © PhotoDisc, Inc. 74 (tr) © PhotoDisc, Inc. 74 (bl) © Artville. 74 (br) © Corbis. 82 (t) © PhotoDisc, Inc. 84 (tl) © PhotoDisc/Getty Images. 84 (tr) © Artville. 84 (bl) © Getty Images/PhotoDisc. 84 (br) © Getty Images/PhotoDisc. 94 (tl) © Siede Preis/PhotoDisc, Inc. 94 (tr) © PhotoDisc, Inc. 94 (bl) © PhotoDisc, Inc. 94 (br) © Ryan McVay/PhotoDisc, Inc. 95-100 (border) © PhotoDisc, Inc. 102 (t) © Corel Stock Photo Library. 102 (b) © Stockbyte/Getty Images. 103 (t) © Getty Images/PhotoDisc. 103 (c) © Getty Images/PhotoDisc. 103 (b) © Getty Images/Digital Vision. 104 (tl) © Stockbyte. 104 (bl) © Digital Vision. 112 (t) © Corbis. 112 (b) © Corbis. 113 (t) © Royalty Free/Corbis. 113 (b) © Corel Stock Photo Library. 114 (tl) © PhotoDisc/Getty Images. 114 (bl) © PhotoDisc, Inc. 114 (br) © Rubber Ball/Getty Images. 122 (t) © Corbis. 122 (b) © Adobe Image Library. 123 (t) © Corbis. 123 (b) © Getty Images/PhotoDisc. 124 (tl) © Eyewire/Getty Images. 124 (tr) © Classic PIO Images. 124 (bl) © Digital Vision. 124 (br) © Masterfile. 132 (t) © Bigshots/Getty Images. 132 (b) © Superstock. 133 (t) © Getty Images. 133 (b) © Corbis. 134 (tl) © PhotoDisc, Inc. 134 (tr) © PhotoDisc, Inc. 134 (bl) © Artville. 134 (br) © PhotoDisc, Inc. 142 (t) © Eyewire. 142 (b) © Photospin. 143 (t) © Corel Stock Photo Library. 143 (b) © Getty Images/PhotoDisc. 144 (tl) © Getty Images/Rubberball Productions. 144 (bl) © Shutterstock. 144 (br) © Alamy. 145 (t) © Getty Images. 145 (bl) © Shutterstock. 145 (border) © Getty Images/Digital Vision. 146-147 (border) © Getty Images/PhotoDisc. 146 (br) © Shutterstock. 148-149 (border) © PhotoDisc/Getty Images. 149 (br) © Shutterstock. 150 (b) © Shutterstock. All other images property of HMH Publishers.